Eblen
Copyright © 2019 Madeleine LaVoie
All rights reserved.

No part of this book may be used
or reproduced in any manner whatsoever
without written permission except
in the case of brief quotations embodied
in critical articles and reviews.

ISBN 978-1-948613-05-7

Sunny Day Publishing, LLC
Cuyahoga Falls, Ohio 44223
www.sunnydaypublishing.com

Printed in the United States of America

EBLEN

By Madeleine LaVoie

Contents

October 2016	6
Love Poem #13	8
Glow	9
My Parents House	10
Rust Belt May	11
So God Damn Soft	12
Chicago	14
New Orleans	15
Real Ghosts	16
Terrible Lover, Wonderful Friend	18
Home/Sick	19
Things I've Found	22
A Word of Advice	24
The Dogs of Leon	25
Victoria	27
Megabus Voyeurism	28
April 2018	30
Texas	31
Abortion Tourism	32
My Phone Died and I Walked	34
Love Poem #15	36
January 2019	38
The House on Willow Street	39
Recalling Spring	41
The Bang at the Ending	43

Home is not a place for me.

Home is a feeling I am always chasing.

It won't stop until I find my space.

This book is a map.

Madeleine LaVoie

October 2016

candy coat me in

camouflage and faux fur

you self appointed prophet

you, tearing apart ideologies and

pulling from the carcass new icons-

a pottery bowl, shattered

a lucky cat necklace, broken

a pack of Pall Mall cigarettes, sinister.

you wrote your autobiography

in the condensation of my car windows

on the way to a tattoo appointment

(I found the bandages buried in my bedsheets,

two weeks too late)

distracted

I play tarot card reader

pressing the page of swords to

smother the petulant prince of whiskey cider

with a Lazarus pendant practically

resting in my cleavage-

too busy scarfing down someone else's vegan

wedding cake

living double lives through half lies

EBLEN

hidden in Metro Parks

and foreign food restaurants

too busy to possibly stop

looking for myself in other people.

Love Poem #13

you told me

my eyes looked green

as you seeped down my esophagus-

cough syrup verde

mindless masturbations of your name

in sing song

with lips laid across

your viridescent throat

purged with

mugwort abortions and

jade smoke

shameful and head hung

hidden in coffee cups

you told me

a lot of things

I'd like to forget

Glow

December

concubine of

cold, quiet rain

linear and even spaced

it has stopped really

"feeling like Christmas"

as clarity turns me robotic

drinking potions from

 paper coffee cups and dirty mason jars

on my attic bedroom floor

binocular eyes focus

on throbbing, luminescent snowflakes

plastic, hung at a house show

yet cannot find my own

upturned lips, scripted

scapegoated for my

impending claustrophobia

I stopped doing yoga-

yogis seem about as calm and collected

as psychiatrists.

Madeleine LaVoie

My Parents House

in the fall
clematis piniculata grows up
through the bedroom window
of my childhood
proper white display
with tasteful green shoots
to hold leftover Labatt Blue bottles
and love letters
muddled and ink stained
but I left in November
and returned a winter two years later
to a similar sterile silence.
My brother
disassociated GPS signal
bench pressed 130 lbs
of resentment
sans empathy
my brother
tears out his hair and hands it to me,
saying
"here, this is guilt
it tastes like oil".

Rust Belt May

rust belt May smells
like fentanyl feels like
sickly sweet Carlo Rossi
in a warehouse full of
 stick-n-poke tattoos
feels like cookies at
family reunions and graduation parties
for cousins you've never met
feels like the red bloom of my toothpaste
spit back into the bathroom sink
clothes stick and cling
to my body in ways that make me
think of my grandpa singing "you are my sunshine"
and pushing me on the swing
make me think about how I
stopped putting pennies heads up
in the soles of my shoes for good luck
how I don't try to remember
being asleep after I wake up anymore.
this is the stage of grief
where we become objects to one another
as a line cook
you'd think I'd be used it
but martyr me
or forget about me, I guess
because you always tell me
you'll talk to me in the morning
when we both know you won't.

Madeleine LaVoie

So God Damn Soft

so
god damn soft that if you
have yet to shove me between
your incisors
and bite down
you're a fucking joke.
I'm waiting for the bluish
purply bruises to show up
a telltale indication of
my spine
breaking through my floral dress
but nothing breaks anymore
it just turns to mush
it is me that is floral
the type of flower you
crush between your fingers
when you step out for a smoke
clichés were something I was more
concerned about avoiding
before I worked 14 hour shifts
to sleep alone at my parents house
how do you write poems
when you have to make a
'campfire mocha'

every five god damn minutes

how do you leave any sort of impression

without lips, hands, thighs

no one taught me

if I'm looking at the sky

I'm faking it

if I'm looking at the ground

I'm thinking about what

I'm going to be when I grow up

probably a bird, a ghost, or

a robot

Chicago

names and numbers

          I wanted to build us a treehouse

are the first to go

          at the edge of town

what was our address?

          with hubcap parapets

where did I work?

          and holiday lights

when you bought loose leaf tobacco

          but by the time that I finally found you

to roll your own cigarettes

          you were already lying

which train did we take home?

          black out drunk

we loaded the U-Haul

          with your hands wrapped around

in the rain

          your own neck

and I think we must have dropped something

          I wanted to build us

in between Logan Square

          a treehouse

and Wicker Park

          at the edge of town

that we've since forgot

          because I thought we might

because sometimes I feel like

          be better off

I could still

          if we were all alone

get off at California

          but we're not.

turn right on West Armitage

left on North Spaulding

walk up three flights of steps

and find you, asleep

New Orleans

I spent three months missing you in Jackson Square,
monogamous monologues thrashing about in my mind
as I knelt crying in Saint Louis Cathedral for hours
the unsentimental eyes of the Catholic monoliths filled
with porcelain contempt. From my tears grew vines of
moonflowers whose tendrils will slowly wrap around
and penetrate the marble
in a thousand years crushing the saints to their feet
swearing to return in spit and blood drawn
with the turquoise pocket knife my brother gave me
the day I turned 20 did not stop over a year from
passing before I smelled the Mississippi river again.
I never found your imprints
of our bodies drawn in white chalk on the Canal
Streetcar, on an empty Bywater corner,
closure a cold case, a comma
a semicolon, at most.

Real Ghosts

the feeling isn't mutual

the feeling is seasonal, now

a summer migration south

disoriented songbird, I have

the wings of a lark

or the feathery hands of an imposter

fingers saran wrapped in insomnia

seek penance, seek an excuse,

seek my clean shaven knees

begging to be

wholesome

a word, a stone swirled

around my mouth

busting all of my teeth

the remnants of childhood superstition

sleeping nude

to ward off ghosts- hypothetically

the ghost would feel embarrassed

averting its gaze from my

prepubescent lily white body

yet I, a real ghost

haunted your bed

EBLEN

drank your coffee, borrowed your

Alex G sweater

my emptiness animal

demanding it be fed things fleshy

until we both hollowed

and I swallowed you

like a pill

nose held, with water

Madeleine LaVoie

Terrible Lover, Wonderful Friend

French exit accented with jasmine and
frankincense- a girl- a half formed curio
in your absence clothed herself in cocaine hangover,
eau de acid stamped with a Michelangelo.
A way stick out her tongue. A girl.
Eyes with wings and fangs.
Bound to sleep in the abandoned cathedral on
the corner of Mandeville or jump a freight train to LA
Valentines Day rose hibiscus k-pin
composed confessions
A girl. A well built war ship from 1927
rudder rusted, I always turn full circle
but by the time I come around
it's always too late.

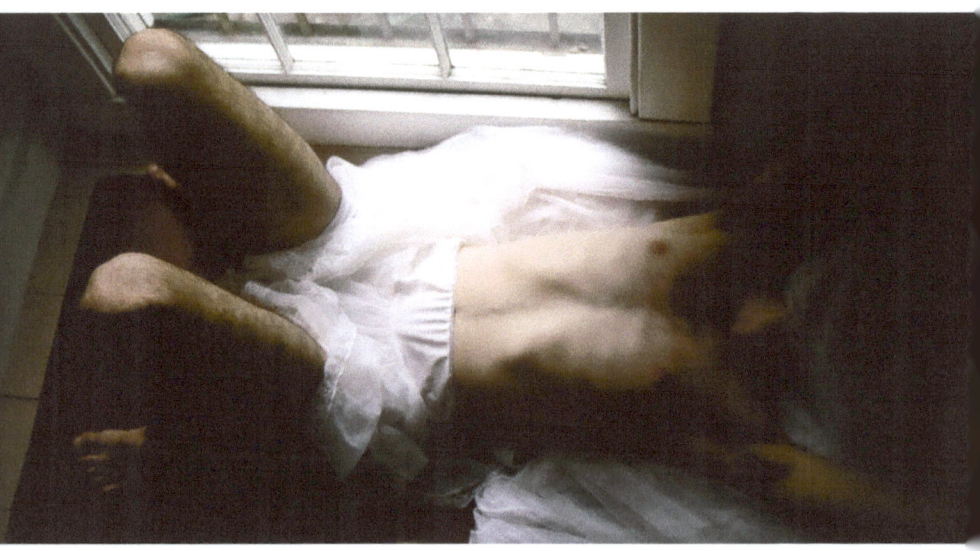

EBLEN

Home/Sick

stubborn nausea

unwilling to subside despite my

best efforts playing witch doctor-

Ohio feathers and Ohio bones bleached

and sewn to the insides of my pockets

spit up from the overgrown golf course

a summer ago

as pine cones crunched beneath my white boots

the latitudes I used to run to

when the street lights came on, 41, 88-

don't fit through the gap

in the mouth of Jefferson Davis Pkwy

don't fit through vacant spaces left

by the teeth that fall out in my dreams

both Jeff Davis and I, we grin like

cowards

holding hands on the rocks

Lake Erie in the dark as

boats sound off in the distance

I ask if they're foghorns and you say "no,

they're just letting one another know

where they are."

Part

Two

Things I've Found

red plastic rosary
rosy crucifixion on the
12 th floor of the library
no cranberry, all vodka
and another dash of faux fur
winter cries cognitive dissonance
held in 3/4 ths empty bottles of red wine
between gloved fingertips,
the midwestern sincerity of desire
of being desired
as more than mere house décor
lost in the small discrepancies
the rosary conceived of the finest Chinese plastic
the blood that does not flow but surges
and recedes at the rate of the heart muscle
and yet
the South
Southern yell of yellow- it
is a denim I stick to
absurd, and bittersweet
lover who only smells human in the morning
who sets their jaw in a way I hate
to look at
who touches the burnt spot on my hand
espresso- machine- steam- wand- casualty
so tenderly, so tender
I bet they could
that really, anyone could
push right through

A Word of Advice

kill your idols

before they want to fuck you

(alternatively… slightly after…)

EBLEN

The Dogs of Leon

in Nicaragua they make eye contact
snap cracking a black rabbit's neck
weightlessly, jaws
smirking
dogs will, after all, be dogs
something I can't stomach as they sleek slip
from beneath porches post meal, nails clicking.
Here, it is hard not to want time
to go too fast beneath the fluorescent lights
my pleas for more made incoherent by a
caffeine intake matched only by that of
recovering alcoholics- our hands curled question
mark style around espresso sin azucar in
every air conditioned cafe in the city.
modeling for a long distance lover I
pose posthumously, our goodbyes
silently emphasized by a "will I
ever see you again"
he tells me he needs to go
all the way gone
in order to come back
in tandem, in incohesive pieces, I wander
head lost in wrappers littered

Madeleine LaVoie

between street corners

the incensed December dances

tinkling faint and far away

and when the dogs show up

frenzied with tongues all lolled out

snorting and lapping at my sore feet

I go with them where they go to sleep

scabby and subdued

EBLEN

Victoria

your name

the way

a loop of thread

is pulled through

by a needle

V for victory

in the rose garden,

a red letter

held between my

thighs like a star

we put the skeleton of

a small animal in my

purse

your name stitched

stem to stem

dripping, dripping

you always stopped

to smell the roses

and I,

looking constantly

skyward,

never really did catch

up

Megabus Voyeurism

round 1

a voyage which begins unsobered
watching the illumination of the cypress skeletons
through the skylight
my father calls me to exclaim
"only the scum of the earth ride buses"
as New Orleans fucks me with jasmine musk
9 feet below sea level
at least this is human faced
at least the spare daffodils and portapotty vampires
aren't sure to remind me I'm the youngest person
in the room every 5 minutes
the graveyard shift driver is a beacon who floods and
fades as I dream up ocean bound airplanes and things
tearing my flesh between two seats
New York, you
museum, mausoleum, monument
to everything we've never been- a new city
each day in the valley of complex concrete and
plexiglass
in one, I get engaged beneath a Fight Club poster
in another, I pinkie swear atop the Coney Island ferris
wheel

round 2

in this version

I die inside a minstrel organ,

pounding on my hip bones in hopes they will show through more and

gripped by phantom pains from a phantom lover

you become me

draw the 9 of swords sleep under 9 dead roses and

carry a headless Saint across at least 3 boroughs then

tell me the moon waxes and wanes without meaning

but if anyone asks, I never

think about ambulances as they go by

"April is the cruelest month of the year"
April 2018

this emptiness wears no clothes.
it is sometimes known as the background noise
that makes up a body
nude, I am the emperor
the half formed thing offering you
a key bump in the 3 am bathroom to say
dreamy and cloudy eyes look the same
Aprils' fool, fragments of unpious desire
Spring forth from the perfect mimicry
of my own bowed head, for years i
fell asleep with my hands clasped but
not a single prayer, just a plea
to be made more mechanical.
this escapism mutters marionette style
invisible thread for miles
begging you to follow your heart
unless it leads here, to me
the me embedded in these words, murmurations
which no longer consist of simply
crawling into the bathtub
with a stolen National Geographic
to touch the glossy images of snakes.

Texas

the small gasp of slipping between

two 16 wheelers,

western manifest destiny

still a madness keeping me

masculine

unable to utter an

I miss you even in all my

billboard faced glory,

even as you laugh rings out more foreign

than any coyote cackle

a juniper whip that hits and runs

I do not speak in names

if butchered,

I fear the blindness

of those binds

eloquence lost in the wrist as

we walk like sleepwalkers,

talk like sleep talkers do

ride over roads which open up like wounds

fester like wounds.

Madeleine LaVoie

Abortion Tourism

June doesn't sleep with me

doesn't settle well in my stomach

peels back my invincibility complex

like wet leather

(at 21, something had to)

a midsummer night's' vacancy

becomes a misused family vacation

orange poppies blooming across Washington State.

the south was far less kind,

lipstick smeared across my wrist like a bird

with a broken wing

my shotgun house standing like glorified driftwood

in a dream I couldn't stand to dream anymore

so

how did I do it?

the med school nosferatu said

I have a high pain tolerance

I wasn't sedated

I never picked up my pharmacy brand oxycontin,

I walked around downtown Seattle until my legs fell

asleep

until i fell asleep

EBLEN

and fragments of me rotted and fell out

dripping honeyless between my thighs,

woke up on a train to San Juan with just

enough time to see the dead cat on the tracks

so I could cover your eyes

and make sure you didn't have to look

Madeleine LaVoie

My Phone Died and I Walked

intimacy and all of its'

slow suffocations

its' bites that bruise much more

the morning after, in the blue hour

when the stores are all bright

but no one stands beneath their reflections

and all the neon crosses blink out.

gathering warmth from a body

that I can't touch

while you hold me inside your head

the filler words hesitate as throat shapes

you ask me to say something no one else

could say to you and I won't.

daily my phone dies

and I never want to revive it

to go off silently is a dream I can't

seem to drown or drive off

besides, the gas tank is always on E and

by the time we eventually try to leave

it's after 5

the LED flickering on on the front porch.

is this really New Orleans?

EBLEN

sometimes I can't stand

to look at it anymore

stray cats we can only feed

with every other paycheck

the busted car AC

but cross your fingers behind your back

pick me up from another house where I

will not fall asleep

run the first stop sign

the second

roll up your windows

and we'll be home.

Love Poem #15

a vanishing act:
you disappear into me
as I disappear, here to
momentarily sop up the
memory stains with this southern
summer slip-n-slide called sex
we soak the sheets
swap sweat and spit
by the mouthful
salty sweet to bitter
a new mouthfeel for me
as love hums on autopilot
next to the air conditioner
and we skin one another
like hunters with our animal pelts
melting off onto the floor.
little thief hands
soot black from dragging along
anything that stands as i walk
they tear at Ms. Stacie's gardenias
sneak into your mouth by the bayou
as the fire ants sting our ankles
c'mon, don't you like the heat?

EBLEN

we blister and you call it a mercy killing

my body dissolving into blue but blue

isn't my color, I want to burn

to the ground for once, tell you

the rose i dropped at your feet

cat- and- prey style was on purpose

i want to show you a goodbye

but all I can ever do is

say "good luck"

Madeleine LaVoie

January 2019

the crisis of another body

leaves me

my jaw, the bottoms of my toes, a neck nape

rough enough to call intentionally cruel

all anatomy going about it's various betrayals again.

sure, you happened to be the worm to do it this time

but I was all overripe peach begging to be

pushed in- my skin a physical delusion

disfigured permanently by bedsheets,

I mean we all know I can't resist a good costume-

the blue and red smears around our mouths like

tiny, colorful defense mechanisms

and besides, your sterile youth rings a bell

a prepubescent voice singing Ring Around the Rosie

your mother and her casual Confederate flags

viewing a hospital from another hospital window

my mother is out working the tollbooths

dreading the day I drive off

and stop really coming back

EBLEN

The House on Willow Street

haint blue porch ceiling painted by praying hands
playing ghost keep- away
yet, by some slip up
there I was, mop of filthy blonde hair
half matted from a former burial
just in time for a round of
who's haunting who.
the vents kissed our ears hissing
invocations of purple pleasure draped
in pleas not to nod off in the driver's seat
anymore, not to go home at all
as if we could! our phantom tongues licking
at the handles and hinges in time with the
drip drip drip of the faucet to no avail.
I found a fox cut in two
in one version of the bedroom
where i held myself hostage
we butterflied eyelashes then I
kicked her under the night stand
that's when i got the idea to drink you
house on Willow Street
like a bottle of warm 7 dollar red wine

Madeleine LaVoie

to line the matches up domino style each morning

until someone struck me

and we all turned to ash

and we all burned down

Recalling Spring

now, the memory comes back

bizarre

we were in New York together

two exhibitionists and someone

who refused to look

we took the L to Chelsea in the freezing rain

fairweather friends who held hands only

after the last subway left the station

what harm could there be

in a trio?

our blue eyes, those noticers

double dealers deemed deceitful

as I feigned damsel in distress

all over his settee

yes, the wretch

was me

determined to be your

candy striper

singing my sickbay songs- why not

spin the bottle

spin out like my Honda CR-V on I-90

last February?

Madeleine LaVoie

the point being

I don't know how to turn around

but at least there's a ritual to it

like Spring- a single dog chewed crocus

me in my knee highs

a Catholic school that left lines on my calves

from there, how did I

triangulate?

the child who cried for each trampled tulip

coming home at 7 am in feathers

and lace red like a smashed fist

with bruised lips grinning and nauseous

but then, the child still desired each

flavor of macaroon, multi-colored tootsie pop mouth

my heart, that awful threesome

could never decide

The Bang at the Ending

when do things start to hurt

more fat lip single punched out

window pane style

less like drowning, as in

the thought of drowning

that makes me wash my hair less frequently.

this body a bruise collector's map

I could point

here, here, here

still warm

pitter pattering across my skin like the footprints

of the saints all the streets are named after

where is the jolt

doggie shock collar around my 12 year old neck

to teach me not to run away style

not disorienting like tumbling off of water skiis

like driving around town pointing out every

house we've lived in.

it's not a matter of falling from grace

me blacked out cursed out lines

of dirty diesel drip

blank faced bad memory faker

Madeleine LaVoie

yes, I toppled

but the bang at the end

where is the bang at the ending?

www.ingramcontent.com/pod-product-compliance
Lightning Source LLC
LaVergne TN
LVHW010030070426
835512LV00004B/54